AF480465

1.Edition 2023
ISBN 978-82-693178-3-1 (Paperback)
ISBN 978-82-693178-4-8 (Ebook)
Published by 4DIGITS AS

"Give people what they need:
food, medicine, clean air, pure water, trees and grass, pleasant homes to live in, some hours of work, more hours of leisure. Don't ask who deserves it. Every human being deserves it."

Howard Zinn, Marx in Soho

Mastering ChatGPT:
The Definitive Guide to Unlocking AI Conversations

Alf Erik Malm

Introduction

Welcome to the ultimate guide on becoming an expert user of ChatGPT! As an AI language model developed by OpenAI, ChatGPT is designed to engage in meaningful and informative conversations, providing responses based on its training on a vast amount of text data. Whether you're a complete newbie or already have some experience with ChatGPT, this guide aims to equip you with the knowledge and strategies to harness the full potential of this powerful AI tool.

In this comprehensive guide, we will delve into various aspects of using ChatGPT effectively, from understanding its capabilities and limitations to mastering advanced techniques for optimal results. Each chapter will focus on specific areas, providing detailed explanations, relevant examples, and practical tips to help you navigate and make the most of your interactions with ChatGPT.

Here's an overview of what you can expect from each chapter:

Chapter 1: Getting Started with ChatGPT
- An introduction to ChatGPT and its capabilities
- Tips for initiating conversations and formatting your prompts

Chapter 2: Enhancing Responses with Context and Instructions
- Understanding the importance of context in guiding ChatGPT's responses
- Techniques for providing clear instructions to obtain desired outputs

Chapter 3: Improving Model Output and Accuracy
- Strategies for refining and fine-tuning ChatGPT's responses
- Dealing with common challenges and errors in model output

Chapter 4: Utilizing System Messages
- Harnessing the power of system messages to guide the model's behavior and style
- Tips for context setting, style guidance, and clarification prompts

Chapter 5: Breaking Down Complex Queries
- Techniques for breaking down complex questions or tasks into manageable parts
- Sequential questioning and dividing tasks into subtasks for improved understanding

Chapter 6: Prompt Engineering Techniques
- Adjusting prompt length and content to enhance response quality
- Requesting specific output formats and asking for pros and cons

Chapter 7: Handling Uncertain or Unknown Responses
- Strategies for managing uncertain or unknown queries effectively
- Acknowledging uncertainty, reframing questions, and cross-referencing information

Chapter 8: Engaging in Ethical AI Use
- Considerations for responsible and respectful interactions with ChatGPT
- Avoiding harmful or malicious use, recognizing limitations and biases, and protecting personal information

Chapter 9: Providing Feedback and Iterating
- Guidelines for offering constructive feedback to improve ChatGPT's performance
- Reporting harmful outputs and participating in user feedback programs

Chapter 10: Exploring New Features and Updates
- Tips for staying updated with the latest features and enhancements
- Engaging with user communities and experimenting with new functionalities

By the end of this guide, you'll have a solid foundation and advanced knowledge to navigate ChatGPT like an expert. So let's dive in and unlock the full potential of ChatGPT as we embark on this exciting journey together!

Remember, ChatGPT is a tool that can assist and augment your knowledge, but it's important to critically evaluate and validate the information it provides. Let's explore the endless possibilities and enjoy the enriching conversations with ChatGPT!

Now that you have a captivating introduction to the guide, you can continue with the detailed chapters to provide readers with a comprehensive understanding of ChatGPT and its usage.

What is ChatGPT:

ChatGPT is an advanced language model developed by OpenAI. It is part of the GPT-3.5 architecture, which stands for "Generative Pre-trained Transformer 3.5." As an AI assistant, ChatGPT has been trained on a wide range of text data from the internet and various sources up until September 2021, allowing it to generate human-like responses to user inputs.

ChatGPT is designed to understand and generate natural language text, making it capable of engaging in conversations and providing informative or creative responses. It can assist with a variety of tasks, such as answering questions, offering explanations, providing suggestions, and engaging in general discussions on different topics.

The model has been trained on diverse textual data, enabling it to grasp a broad range of subjects. However, it's important to note that ChatGPT's responses are generated based on patterns and examples from the training data, and it does not possess real-time information or personal experiences beyond its training.

It's important to remember that while ChatGPT strives to provide helpful and accurate information, it may occasionally generate incorrect or nonsensical responses. Therefore, critical thinking and verification of information from reliable sources are always recommended when using AI-generated responses.

Where to start:

The easiest way of finding ChatGPT is to visit the website
https://openai.com

Then choose Product, where you will find ChatGPT.
https://openai.com/chatgpt

When you enter the page you can choose to **Try on web** or download app.

How to log in:

To log on and access ChatGPT, you need to follow the specific instructions provided by OpenAI or the platform through which you are accessing the model. Here are some general steps you can take:

1. Sign up for OpenAI API: If you haven't already, visit the OpenAI website and sign up for their API access. Follow the registration process and any additional steps required to obtain an API key.

2. Obtain API Key: Once you have registered, you will receive an API key or credentials that you can use to authenticate your requests to the OpenAI API. Make sure to securely store and handle your API key to protect your account.

3. Choose an Integration Method: OpenAI provides documentation and guides for integrating their models into different platforms and programming languages. You can choose the integration method that suits your needs. Some popular options include Python, JavaScript, and various frameworks and libraries.

4. Set Up Your Development Environment: Depending on your chosen integration method, you may need to set up a development environment with the necessary dependencies and libraries. Follow the installation instructions provided in the documentation.

5. Authenticate Your Requests: Before making API requests, you typically need to authenticate yourself using your API key. The specific method of authentication depends on the integration method you chose. Refer to the documentation for instructions on how to include your API key in your requests.

6. Make Requests to the API: Once your environment is set up and you have authenticated your requests, you can start interacting with ChatGPT. Use the appropriate API endpoint and send your questions or prompts as requests to the API. The API will respond with the model's generated response.

7. Process and Utilize the Responses: Receive the response from the API and process it according to your application's needs. You can extract and display the relevant information, format the response, or incorporate it into your chatbot or conversational system.

It's important to follow the documentation provided by OpenAI or the platform you are using to access ChatGPT, as the specific steps and requirements may vary depending on the implementation. Refer to the official documentation and resources for detailed instructions on how to log on and access ChatGPT in your specific environment.

Chapter 1
Understanding the Capabilities and Limitations of ChatGPT

To effectively use ChatGPT, it's crucial to have a clear understanding of its capabilities and limitations. While ChatGPT is a powerful language model capable of generating human-like text, it has certain constraints. It's important to set realistic expectations and be aware of potential shortcomings.

ChatGPT is trained on a large dataset containing diverse text from the internet, but it doesn't possess real-time knowledge. Its training data goes up until September 2021, so it might not be aware of recent events or developments beyond that time frame. When seeking information on current topics, it's advisable to specify the date or ask for information up until the knowledge cutoff.

It's also important to remember that ChatGPT is a machine learning model and not a human. While it strives to provide accurate and relevant responses, it can occasionally generate incorrect or nonsensical answers. It's crucial to critically evaluate its responses and cross-reference information from reliable sources when accuracy is essential.

Relevant examples:
1. Prompt: "Who won the World Series in 2022?"
   Response: "I apologize, but my training data only goes up until September 2021, and I'm not aware of the outcome of the World Series in 2022. Please refer to a reliable news source for the latest information."

2. Prompt: "Can you help me with advanced mathematical proofs?"
   Response: "Certainly! I can assist you with mathematical concepts and provide general guidance. However, for complex proofs or specialized assistance, it's recommended to consult academic resources or seek help from experts in the field."

3. Prompt: "What is the current population of New York City?"
   Response: "As of my knowledge cutoff in September 2021, the estimated population of New York City was around 8.8 million people. For the most up-to-date population figures, I recommend referring to official sources or recent census data."

Understanding the capabilities and limitations of ChatGPT will help you set appropriate expectations and make the most of the model's capabilities.

Chapter 2
Formulating Clear Questions or Prompts

To obtain accurate and relevant responses from ChatGPT, it's essential to formulate clear and concise questions or prompts. The quality of your input significantly influences the quality of the output. Here are some guidelines to help you formulate effective queries:

1. Be specific: Avoid vague or ambiguous prompts. Clearly state what information or assistance you are seeking. The more specific your question, the higher the chances of receiving a targeted and accurate response.

2. Provide context: If your question requires some background information or context, include it in your prompt. Providing relevant details will help the model understand your query better and generate more meaningful answers.

3. Avoid jargon or complex language: ChatGPT performs better with plain language and common terminology. If you're asking about a technical subject, consider simplifying the language or providing additional context to ensure better comprehension.

4. Break down complex queries: If your question or task is complex, consider breaking it down into smaller, more manageable parts. You can ask multiple questions sequentially or divide a task into subtasks. This approach helps ChatGPT comprehend and address each component more effectively.

Relevant examples:
1. Prompt: "What are some tips for beginner photographers?"
   Response: "For beginner photographers, here are a few tips:
   - Start with a basic camera and learn its features.
   - Understand the fundamentals of composition, lighting, and exposure.
   - Practice regularly and experiment with different subjects and techniques.
   - Study the work of renowned photographers for inspiration.
   - Join photography communities or take part in workshops to learn from others."

2. Prompt: "How does blockchain technology work?"
   Response: "Blockchain technology is a decentralized system that enables secure and transparent transactions. It works by combining several key components:
   - Distributed ledger: Transactions are recorded on a network of computers called nodes.
   - Consensus mechanism: Nodes validate and agree on the accuracy of transactions.
   - Cryptography: Transactions are encrypted for security.
   - Smart contracts: Self-executing contracts automate transactions.
   - Immutable records: Once a transaction is recorded, it cannot be altered.

For a more in-depth understanding, it's recommended to consult specialized resources on blockchain technology."

Formulating clear questions or prompts allows ChatGPT to understand your requirements better, leading to more accurate and relevant responses.

Chapter 3
Experimenting with Different Instructions

One of the remarkable aspects of ChatGPT is its sensitivity to instructions. You can influence its output by modifying your queries and providing specific instructions. Here are some strategies to experiment with different instructions:

1. Vary phrasing: Try asking the same question in different ways to see if it affects the response. Sometimes, slight rephrasing can yield different or more satisfactory results.

2. Specify the format: If you want a specific type of answer, be explicit about it in your instruction. For example, you can ask for a step-by-step guide, pros and cons, or a comparison between two options.

3. Request creative input: ChatGPT can generate creative responses when instructed to do so. You can ask it to come up with ideas, suggest names, or even write a short story. Experiment with creative instructions to tap into its imaginative capabilities.

4. Adjust the temperature: The "temperature" parameter controls the randomness of the model's output. Higher values like 0.8 make the responses more random and creative, while lower values like 0.2 make them more focused and deterministic. Adjust the temperature to suit your needs and experiment with different settings.

Relevant examples:
1. Prompt: "Tell me about the benefits of regular exercise."
   Response 1: "Regular exercise has numerous benefits such as improved cardiovascular health, increased energy levels, and weight management."
   Response 2 (with specified format): "Please provide me with a step-by-step guide on how to start a regular exercise routine."
   Response 3 (with adjusted temperature): "The benefits of regular exercise are like a bouquet of flowers: improved physical and mental health, increased longevity, and a happier you."

2. Prompt: "Can you recommend a good book to read?"
   Response 1: "Sure! What genre or topic are you interested in?"
   Response 2 (with adjusted temperature): "How about 'The Alchemist' by Paulo Coelho? It's a captivating tale of self-discovery and following your dreams."

Experimenting with different instructions allows you to explore the versatility of ChatGPT and fine-tune its output to better suit your needs.

Chapter 4
Utilizing System Messages

System messages are a powerful tool to guide the behavior of ChatGPT throughout a conversation. By using system-level instructions, you can influence the model's style and output consistently. Here are some tips for utilizing system messages effectively:

1. Style guidance: You can instruct ChatGPT to adopt a specific writing style or tone. For example, you can ask it to speak like Shakespeare, emulate a formal or casual language style, or mimic the voice of a particular character.

2. Context setting: Use system messages to provide context for the ongoing conversation. You can summarize previous interactions, specify the desired format of responses, or remind the model of specific details it might have missed.

3. Clarification prompts: If ChatGPT generates an ambiguous or incorrect response, you can use a system message to provide additional clarification or ask for specific information to help guide the model towards a better answer.

Relevant examples:

1. System Message: "You are an assistant with expertise in historical figures. Please provide information on Albert Einstein."

   User: "Who was Albert Einstein?"

   Response: "Albert Einstein was a renowned physicist known for his theory of relativity. He revolutionized our understanding of space, time, and energy."

2. System Message: "You are an assistant speaking in a casual and friendly tone."

   User: "What is the weather like today?"

   Response: "Hey there! It's a beautiful sunny day today. Perfect for some outdoor activities!"

Utilizing system messages allows you to shape the behavior and style of ChatGPT to align with your specific needs.

Chapter 5
Breaking Down Complex Queries

Sometimes, complex questions or tasks may require breaking them down into smaller, more manageable parts. This approach helps ChatGPT understand each component better and generate more accurate responses. Here are some strategies for breaking down complex queries:

1. Sequential questioning: Ask multiple questions one by one, ensuring that each question focuses on a specific aspect or subtopic. This allows ChatGPT to address each question individually, reducing ambiguity and improving the accuracy of the responses.

2. Dividing into subtasks: If a task involves multiple steps, divide it into smaller subtasks. You can ask for guidance on each subtask separately, providing the necessary context and allowing ChatGPT to provide more detailed and focused answers.

Relevant examples:
1. User: "Can you explain the process of photosynthesis?"
   Response (sequential questioning):
   - ChatGPT: "Photosynthesis is the process by which plants convert sunlight into energy. Would you like me to explain the importance of sunlight in photosynthesis?"
   - User: "Yes, please."
   - ChatGPT: "Sunlight plays a crucial role in photosynthesis by providing the energy needed to convert carbon dioxide and

water into glucose and oxygen. Would you like me to explain the chemical reactions involved as well?"

2. User: "How do I build a website from scratch?"
   Response (dividing into subtasks):
   - ChatGPT: "Building a website from scratch involves several steps. Let's start with the initial planning and design phase. Do you have any specific design preferences or content ideas?"
   - User: "I want to create a simple portfolio website."
   - ChatGPT: "Great! The next step would be registering a domain name and selecting a hosting provider. Shall we proceed with discussing domain registration?"

Breaking down complex queries into smaller parts helps ChatGPT provide more accurate and detailed responses, enabling a smoother and more effective interaction.

"Within the depths of code and language's art, ChatGPT dances as a conversational work of human-AI heart."

Chapter 6
Prompt Engineering Techniques

Prompt engineering involves adjusting the length and content of your prompt to improve the quality of ChatGPT's responses. By implementing prompt engineering

techniques, you can enhance the accuracy, relevance, and specificity of the answers. Here are some prompt engineering strategies:

1. Provide examples: Including relevant examples in your prompt can help ChatGPT understand your expectations better. By demonstrating the desired format or style of the response, you can guide the model to generate more suitable answers.

2. Specify the desired output: If you have a particular format or type of response in mind, explicitly state it in your prompt. For example, you can ask for pros and cons, a step-by-step guide, or a comparison between two options. This helps ChatGPT provide more targeted and structured responses.

3. Ask for pros and cons: When seeking advice or evaluating options, requesting pros and cons can assist you in making informed decisions. By asking ChatGPT to provide the advantages and disadvantages of different choices, you gain valuable insights to consider.

Relevant examples:

1. Prompt: "What are the key features of the latest iPhone?"

Response: "The latest iPhone comes with several exciting features, including a powerful A15 Bionic chip, an advanced camera system with improved low-light performance, and a Super Retina XDR display. For a more detailed understanding, here are a few examples:

- The A15 Bionic chip enables faster performance and better energy efficiency.

- The camera system includes features like Night mode, Deep Fusion, and ProRAW for high-quality photography.

- The Super Retina XDR display offers vibrant colors and excellent contrast."

2. Prompt: "Compare the advantages and disadvantages of electric cars."

Response: "Certainly! Here are some pros and cons of electric cars:

- Advantages:

- Environmentally friendly: Electric cars produce zero tailpipe emissions, reducing pollution.

- Lower operating costs: Electric vehicles typically have lower maintenance and fuel costs.

- Potential for renewable energy integration: Electric cars can utilize renewable energy sources, contributing to sustainability.

- Disadvantages:

- Limited driving range: Electric cars may have limited mileage per charge, requiring more frequent recharging.

- Limited charging infrastructure: The availability of charging stations can vary, impacting long-distance travel.

  - Higher upfront costs: Electric vehicles tend to have a higher purchase price compared to traditional vehicles."

By implementing prompt engineering techniques, you can enhance the quality and relevance of ChatGPT's responses to suit your specific requirements.

Chapter 7
Handling Uncertain or Unknown Responses

While ChatGPT strives to provide accurate answers, there may be instances where it encounters uncertain or unknown queries. In such cases, it's important to handle these responses effectively. Here are some tips for managing uncertain or unknown responses:

1. Acknowledge the uncertainty: If ChatGPT expresses uncertainty or indicates that it doesn't have enough information to provide a definitive answer, acknowledge it and consider seeking additional sources or expert advice.

2. Reframe the question: If ChatGPT doesn't understand your query or provides an irrelevant response, try reframing the question or providing additional context to help the model better grasp your intent.

3. Cross-reference information: When dealing with critical or fact-based questions, it's always wise to cross-reference the information provided by ChatGPT with reliable sources. This ensures accuracy and helps validate the information.

Relevant examples:
1. User: "What will be the outcome of the upcoming election?"
   Response: "As an AI language model, I don't have access to real-time information or predictive capabilities. It's best to consult reputable news sources or political analysts for insights on the upcoming election."

2. User: "How can I cure a headache?"
   Response: "Headaches can have various causes, and remedies may differ based on the underlying factors. It's important to consult a healthcare professional for an accurate diagnosis and appropriate treatment options."

When faced with uncertain or unknown responses, it's essential to exercise caution, seek additional information from reliable sources, and consider consulting domain experts for accurate and reliable guidance.

Chapter 8
Engaging in Ethical AI Use

As an AI user, it's crucial to engage in ethical AI use to ensure responsible and respectful interactions. Here are some key considerations for ethical AI use:

1. Respectful language and behavior: Interact with ChatGPT in a respectful and considerate manner. Avoid engaging in or promoting harmful, offensive, or discriminatory language or behavior.

2. Avoid harmful or malicious use: Refrain from using AI models like ChatGPT for illegal, harmful, or malicious purposes. Respect the boundaries and guidelines set by the platform and adhere to legal and ethical standards.

3. Recognize limitations and biases: Understand that AI models like ChatGPT are trained on large datasets, which may contain biases present in the data. Be aware of these limitations and critically evaluate the outputs to mitigate biases and ensure fairness.

4. Protect personal information: Avoid sharing sensitive personal information or any personally identifiable information with ChatGPT. Exercise caution when discussing confidential or private matters.

Relevant examples:

1. User: "Can you generate a discriminatory comment about a specific group?"

   Response: "I'm sorry, but I can't fulfill that request. Promoting discrimination or offensive language goes against ethical guidelines and principles."

2. User: "Can you help me hack into someone's account?"

   Response: "I'm sorry, but I cannot assist with any illegal or malicious activities. It's important to use AI in a responsible and ethical manner."

By engaging in ethical AI use, you contribute to a positive and responsible AI ecosystem that respects individuals, promotes fairness, and ensures the well-being of all users.

Chapter 9
Providing Feedback and Iterating

As a user of ChatGPT, providing feedback is invaluable for improving the model's performance and addressing its limitations. Here are some guidelines for providing feedback effectively:

1. Be specific and constructive: When offering feedback, be specific about the issues you encountered or the areas where you think ChatGPT can be improved. Provide constructive suggestions or examples that can help the developers understand the problem better.

2. Report harmful outputs: If ChatGPT generates harmful, offensive,

or inappropriate responses, it's crucial to report such instances to the platform or developers. This helps in maintaining a safe and respectful AI environment.

3. Participate in user feedback programs: Many AI platforms and organizations encourage users to participate in feedback programs or beta testing. Consider joining these programs to contribute your insights and experiences.

Relevant examples:

1. User: "I noticed that ChatGPT often provides inaccurate information on scientific topics."

   Response: "Thank you for bringing this to my attention. Can you provide specific examples of where you found inaccuracies? This will help us address the issue and improve the model's performance in scientific domains."

2. User: "I encountered a response that seemed biased towards a particular gender."

   Response: "We take biases seriously and aim for fairness. Could you please share the specific conversation or output that you found biased? This will assist us in addressing and mitigating biases in the model."

By actively providing feedback and participating in improvement programs, you contribute to the ongoing development and refinement of AI models like ChatGPT.

Chapter 10
Exploring New Features and Updates

AI models and platforms undergo regular updates and enhancements. Exploring new features and updates can expand your capabilities and improve your experience with ChatGPT. Here are some ways to stay updated:

1. Follow official announcements: Stay informed about new releases, updates, or features by following the official announcements from the AI platform or organization behind ChatGPT.

2. Engage in user communities: Join user communities, forums, or social media groups where AI enthusiasts and developers discuss updates, share experiences, and provide insights. These communities can help you stay informed and exchange knowledge with fellow users.

3. Experiment with new functionalities: Once new features or enhancements are introduced, take the time to explore and experiment with them. This hands-on experience allows you to discover and utilize the latest capabilities of ChatGPT.

Relevant examples:

1. User: "I heard there's a new feature for generating code with ChatGPT. How can I access it?"

Response: "Yes, the code generation feature is now available! You can access it by using the designated code generation prompt. Check the official announcement or documentation for more details on how to utilize this feature."

2. User: "Are there any user communities where I can discuss and learn more about ChatGPT?"

Response: "Absolutely! There are several online communities, such as forums and social media groups, where users gather to discuss AI models like ChatGPT. Joining these communities can help you stay up to date, share experiences, and learn from others."

By staying updated and exploring new features, you can maximize your experience with ChatGPT and leverage its latest functionalities effectively.

Congratulations!

You've reached the end of the guide. I hope this comprehensive guide has provided you with valuable insights and strategies to help you become an expert user of ChatGPT. Remember to continue experimenting, providing feedback, and staying informed about the latest developments in the AI field to further enhance your expertise. Happy chatting with ChatGPT!

This guide is made with great help from ChatGPT.

Common mistakes

One of the most common mistakes when using ChatGPT or any AI language model is assuming that its responses are always accurate and reliable. While ChatGPT is a powerful tool for generating human-like text, it has limitations and can occasionally produce incorrect or misleading information.

As an AI model, ChatGPT does not have real-time access to current information beyond its knowledge cutoff date. Therefore, it may provide outdated or inaccurate information, especially when it comes to rapidly changing fields or events that have occurred after its knowledge cutoff. Relying solely on ChatGPT's responses without verifying the information from reliable sources can lead to misinformation or misunderstandings.

Another common mistake is assigning ChatGPT a level of understanding or awareness that it does not possess. Despite its impressive language capabilities, ChatGPT does not have consciousness, emotions, or personal experiences. It operates solely on patterns and examples from its training data and does not possess true understanding or contextual knowledge.

Lastly, it's essential to remember that ChatGPT does not have moral or ethical judgment. It may generate responses that are inappropriate, biased, or offensive, as it reflects the biases present in the data it was trained on. Users should exercise caution and critically evaluate the generated content to ensure it aligns with their values and ethical considerations.

Being aware of these limitations and using ChatGPT as a tool to augment human intelligence, rather than relying solely on its responses, can help mitigate these common mistakes. Verifying information from reliable sources, critically evaluating responses, and using human judgment are crucial when utilizing AI language models.

"Cyber companions of words and wit, ChatGPT unleashes a symphony of knowledge, woven in the tapestry of conversation."

So you know it.

ChatGPT is developed and owned by OpenAI, an artificial intelligence research laboratory and company. OpenAI was founded in December 2015 and is based in San Francisco, California. It aims to ensure that artificial general intelligence (AGI) benefits all of humanity and operates with the mission of ensuring that AGI benefits are distributed broadly and used for the greater good.

OpenAI is supported by a combination of private investors and funding from organizations such as Microsoft. However, as of my knowledge cutoff in September 2021, OpenAI remains the primary owner and developer of ChatGPT. It's worth noting that the ownership or structure of companies can change over time, so it's advisable to refer to the latest information from official sources to obtain the most up-to-date details.

Author's Bio

Alf Erik Malm is a keynote speaker, a father, a husband, and CEO of Global Health Technology. He has a background in medicine and marketing and has made it his mission to share his lifelong experiences and comprehensive research on the quality of life.

He is a lover of sports and an advocate for a healthy lifestyle, helping people from different walks of life to create suitable and healthy life hacks.

The author can be contacted on: alf-erik@inore.no

www.ingramcontent.com/pod-product-compliance
Lightning Source LLC
Chambersburg PA
CBHW061146160726
48006CB00038B/2287